Goodbye Singleness

Karen-Marie Gariba

Legal Disclaimer

ISBN: 978-1-7779784-0-2
Published by: Karen-Marie Gariba

Unless otherwise marked, scriptures are taken from the NEW AMERICAN STANDARD BIBLE®, Copyright © 1960, 1962, 1963, 1968, 1971, 1972, 1973, 1975, 1977, 1995 by The Lockman Foundation. Used by permission.

Scripture quotations marked (NIV) are taken from THE HOLY BIBLE, NEW INTERNATIONAL VERSION®, NIV© Copyright © 1973, 1978, 1984, 2011 by Biblica, Inc.® Used by permission. All rights reserved worldwide.

Scripture quotations marked (GNT) are from the Good News Translation in Today's English Version- Second Edition Copyright © 1992 by American Bible Society. Used by Permission.

Gariba Ministries International www.gariba.org karenmarie@gariba.org

Early reviews

"After reading this gem, my heart is softer, my hope is invigorated and my faith is emboldened."

Ayesha Fritz, Oklahoma, USA

"A journey of the heart across continents and nations … a real life love story that is relatable for all women."

Kiwanda Redner, "Immersed" Author

"Such an inspirational love story of waiting for and praying in God's best for you."

Lia Partridge, Ontario, Canada

"A love story that will make you believe in love"

Pastor Zak Gariba

Dedication

I would like to dedicate this book to my loving, wonderful husband and life partner, Zak Gariba.

I thank God for you, and I thank Him for the amazing journey He had us on in these pages, and continues to have us on.

To God who put this love story together.

And to my Mam.

Acknowledgements

There are so many people I would like to thank who have been a blessing on this journey.

My wonderful husband Zak for his love and support.

Our amazing son Zak Jr. for being such a blessing.

My Mam and Dad and my sisters for their love and kindness.

Dear friends who have been a special part of this journey - Elizabeth Hames, Nicole Epp, Florence Joseph, Kiwanda Redner, Carolyn Soldano and Kathy Cook.

Pastor Roger and Sheila for being a part of this story and for being a part of this book.

Grant and Marilyn Holditch for all their help with this book.

Pastors Jamie and Christine Tonge for being a part of this story.

My four praying friends in Hong Kong.

Our pastors Jerry and Pam Steingard.

Thank you to the whole Jubilee Celebration Centre church family.

Janet Tonello of Lakeside Graphics for the design.

Gracii Partridge for photography.

Also thank you to my advance reader team, and to all who have kept, and continue to keep this book in prayer 🖤

Foreword

The story about our relationship is like a fairy tale, like a movie. But this is a real life romance from the beginning. Our lives are going to be a testament for others to learn from.

The real life story about a girl from Shetland who went to Hong Kong and then to Canada, and a man from Africa's Ghana, and how they met at school in Canada.

How God set us up from the moment we met in school till our first date was unusual. A love story that will make you believe in love.

Table of Contents

Preface

Find a comfy spot, and a quiet moment, and read with a warm cuppa on your couch, with a close friend over brunch, or using the simple summary notes at the back, as a small group with your sisters in faith.

I share my story as a simple coffee time chat. One sister to another. I pray that in these pages you will find hope, encouragement and inspiration, and most of all love.

Much love 🖤

Introduction

My husband knocked it out of the park and took my breath away when I read what he had written for the foreword of this book.

Yes, I felt to share my story as an inspiration and encouragement for those waiting and praying for their husband.

Yes, to sharing some simple keys I had learned along the way …

But as the early reviews began coming in for my book, I started to come to the realization that my story was doing something more …

"… loved your book" …

"… my heart is softer …"

" … this book will touch so many …"

I had trusted God in the *living* of this story … and now it seemed He was also doing something in the *writing* of this story …

He was touching hearts …

I tried to seek God for each stage of how He wanted this book to come together and I heard the distinct, still, small voice of the Lord, that I was to ask my husband to write a "word from Zak" at the beginning of the book, which became the foreword for this book. I was so impacted by it that it became the quote on the front cover.

A love story that will make you believe in love.

I think my husband's words have captured the very heart of this God love story so well.

My prayer, our prayer, is that in these pages you will find inspiration and encouragement, learn some simple keys for your own journey, and that, indeed, you will find "a love story that will make you believe in love".

Chapter 1: Pray with

"God, bring us together… from the north, south, east and west" a simple prayer of four single girls at a brunch at a Mexican restaurant in the Mid-Levels district of Hong Kong.

God had already brought us to the amazing city of Hong Kong. So it seemed entirely conceivable that He could also bring us together with our future husbands.

How did I find myself, born and raised in Scotland, as a single woman living and working in Hong Kong?

That is quite a story in itself, the story of my travels around the world, a story I hope to share in a future book.

This book will focus on my journey from starting to pray for my future husband to meeting the man I would marry.

That brunch prayer session that started as a one-time meeting became a weekly occurrence.

The support, encouragement, company and sisterhood of these gals was something I will always cherish. Do you have special friends in your life?

We had precious, precious times together; hiking, meals, restaurants, movies, and even world travels.

And we prayed.

The first tip I would give is to find someone, or some people, with whom to pray.

> *Again I say to you, that if two of you agree*
> *on earth about anything that they may ask, it*
> *shall be done for them by My Father who is*
> *in heaven." Matthew 18:19*

So we agreed with each other and for each other. We prayed from the heart because we understood each other's situation.

> *Do two walk together unless they have*
> *agreed to do so?" Amos 3:3 (NIV)*

The Bible talks about encouraging one another.

Therefore encourage one another and build up one another, just as you also are doing."
1 Thessalonians 5:11

Mutual encouragement was unquestionably a strength of our group. Throughout that time, we were there for one another, supporting each other.

Two of the girls were born in New Zealand. One was a Hong Kong gal, but her family was back in New Zealand. I was from Scotland. So we were family for each other, for birthdays, Easter and even some Christmases. It was only at the very end of our time in Hong Kong that I almost had a Christmas alone.

The four of us prayed together powerfully and specifically, in agreement for one another.

So what did we pray for?

Each week was different, but the same themes came up again and again and again.

Bless Him

It wasn't some kind of pie-in-the-sky prayer. I wasn't praying for a phantom, a mystery person. I was praying for a real person.

A story I heard one time helped me get the right lens for it. A person met a world-famous celebrity on an airplane. He said to the famous person, "I just can't believe you are here!" The superstar said with a smile, "Well, I have to be somewhere, so it might as well be right here."

That helped me to get my perspective—he's out there. I may not have met him yet, but he is out there. So, in addition to asking God to bless him and prepare him, pray for him as a real person.

Are you ready to start praying for him, as a real person?

Bring us together from the north, south, east and west

That might have been all the more evident for us, as we were already living in a foreign land. However, I believe it's true for each one of us. It may be for him to move; it may be for you to move, or perhaps for both of you to move, as it was for me and my future husband.

It may be moving around the globe or only moving around the corner. Your future spouse may be in your circle right now. Possibly it is not even a physical move but rather a moving of hearts.

Are you willing to follow God as He leads?

God prepare me

How? Any great course available, or some good class to attend. Sign me up!

I figured the more I could do to prepare myself, the better it would be for my life and my future marriage. And so I prepared. Was I perfect? No, not at all. Still, I tried to deal with any issues in my heart, growing in Christ during that season and the following seasons.

Are you willing to pray a simple prayer "Lord, prepare me …"?

During this period of pressing into God for my growth as a Christian, I received some promises from God. More on that in the next chapter.

Chapter 2: Promise

T he Bible is full of promises.

But there's something special about His promise to you. Have you ever experienced His special promise to you?

The Bible tells us all His promises are "Yes and Amen" in Christ Jesus. So yes, there are promises for each of us. But there's something so special, so sweet about His promise to us individually that it makes our heart soar and makes our heart sing.

I will share the promises God has given me and the particular scriptures He spoke to me during my season of waiting and praying. But I encourage you to seek God for His promises to you.

It can come through Bible reading, prayer, a prophetic word or through a dream.

But the main thing is when you get it, get it on the inside of you …

Memorize it.

Meditate on it.

Quote It.

Remind yourself of it.

And remind God of it.

Keep it at the front of your remembrance.

God gave me three significant promises about my future husband. I could take you to the exact spot where I encountered God and received each one.

The First Promise

I was at a church service in Shetland. It was Christmas time. If you are single, waiting for your husband, that can be one of the hardest times.

I had been up at the altar to receive prayer and returned back to my seat. I was just having a quiet moment with the Lord.

An older gentleman in the congregation approached me and gently said, "Karen, I believe I have a word from the Lord for you."

He was a quiet man, and in all the time I have known him, this was the first time I had seen him come forward with a prophetic word. My interest was piqued. I listened as he continued, "Would that be okay if I give it to you?" I smiled and nodded my head, "Yes, yes, of course, thank you."

"This is the verse the Lord gave me for you." He opened his Bible and read the words to me:

> *Delight yourself also in the Lord; And He*
> *shall give you the desires of your heart.*
> *Commit your way to the Lord, Trust also in*
> *Him, and He will do it. Psalm 37:4-5*

And then he did something very significant: he didn't add to it.

He said, "I don't know what promise it is, but I felt the Lord say that you would know." I thanked him and nodded, for indeed I did know. And he was on his way.

Tears filled my eyes and started to flow down my cheeks. Indeed, yes, I knew which desire he was talking about.

There, on an ordinary Sunday, just sitting on my chair at church, the God of heaven had swooped down and deposited a promise in my heart. My heart was full.

One of the verses in the Bible talks about the seed:

> *And He spoke many things to them in parables, saying, "Behold, the sower went out to sow; and as he sowed, some seeds fell beside the road, and the birds came and ate them up". Matthew 13:3-4*

Have you received a promise from God through a prophetic word?

Write those words down. Share them with those you trust for prayer and accountability.

When sharing words that you have received, my encouragement to you is to use wisdom with whom to share, and when. If you receive a word in your heart that you sense is from the Lord, share it deeply, only with those you trust, and don't scatter those seeds too widely.

The Second Promise

The second significant promise the Lord gave me was when He spoke to me through the Word of God. I could take you to the spot and to the moment.

My sister had come to visit me in Hong Kong, and we had gone on holiday together to Thailand. I was out on the balcony, reading my Good News Bible that someone had given me as a new believer.

As a new Christian, I was reading the words for the first time. Still, I assure you God can highlight His scripture, bringing it to life whether reading it the first time or the one-hundredth or even the one-thousandth time

Search in the LORD's book of living creatures and read what it says. Not one of these creatures will be missing, and not one will be without its mate. The LORD has commanded it to be so; he himself will bring them together. Isaiah 34:16 (GNT)

He had spoken a promise to me and deposited an assurance in me. The words leapt off the page: "would not be without its mate… "

He promised that He would bring them together, a promise that He would bring me together with my husband.

… will bring them together ... Isaiah 34:16 (GNT)

My God had spoken to me, alone on that balcony. I had encountered God.

I treasured that scripture from Isaiah, a precious promise my God had personally given me.

It was all the more valued as this was not a widely read scripture—and it was quoted in the right way for me to hear it in the Good News Bible.

It was a promise to me, and my heart was full.

Hmmm, He would bring them together …

Have you received a promise from God's Word?

One of the lessons we can learn from the Bible is from Mary. She had been given a promise. In the book of Luke, we read:

> *But Mary treasured all these things,*
> *pondering them in her heart. Luke 2:19*

I am a scripture "quoter," but not that much of a scripture "memorizer". However, I took Isaiah's scripture deep into my memory and deep into my heart. Just before the launch of this book, while being interviewed on an online broadcast about my story, I quoted the verse without even looking at it.

How, you might ask? I didn't need to look for it externally on paper — I already had it printed internally on my heart.

So I treasured it.

And I pondered it.

And I believed it.

He would bring us together.

What could that mean?

I encourage you to treasure, ponder, and believe any word of promise you receive from God.

The Third Promise

My four praying friends and I were on a retreat at the Hyatt Regency in Macau, a Portuguese enclave near Hong Kong.

We had a wonderful time travelling together, eating together, and, of course, praying together.

We were at a side area outdoors, under some lattice pagoda shading. We each had open Bibles, sharing and praying with one another. My eyes were drawn to a passage in the Song of Songs:

> *Put me like a seal over your heart,*
>
> *Like a seal on your arm.*
>
> *For love is as strong as death,*
>
> *Jealousy is as severe as Sheol;*
>
> *Its flashes are flashes of fire,*
>
> *The very flame of the LORD.*
>
> *Many waters cannot quench love,*
>
> *Nor will rivers overflow it;*
>
> *If a man were to give all the riches of his house for love,*
>
> *It would be utterly despised. Song of Solomon 8:6-7*

Mesmerized by the scripture, I lifted my eyes to my friends gathered together. I exclaimed, "I think

God just gave me a promise that my marriage is going to be powerful."

Has God spoken a word to you about your future marriage?

My third promise had just been deposited in my heart.

My faith continued to grow. Surely, God would bring me together with my future husband.

We spent our weekend together praying for each other as usual. But this time, even more so, with our prolonged time at the hotel.

Prayer times were powerful. Each of us received healing and freedom through the laying on of hands.

And then I did something I've never done before: I stayed on by myself for an extra day of personal retreat. I was about to encounter God in a special way.

Single or married, we are all loved, valued and called by God.

"But each of you has your own gift from God, one has this gift, another has that" 1 Corinthians 7:7 (NIV)

Seek God for His promise to you.

Have you ever taken some time away for a personal retreat? A quiet time for you to meet alone with God? It could be an overnight, or simply a day away to a quiet, tranquil spot for prayer and seeking God. It is something that has been a blessing in my life. If you haven't had a short personal retreat yet, I encourage you to seek God and give it a try ...

"For I know the plans that I have for you," declares the LORD, "plans for welfare and not for calamity to give you a future and a hope." Jeremiah 29:11

Karen-Marie Gariba

Chapter 3: Priorities

Praying for, thinking of, and hoping for my husband, were these all good? Yes, by all means. But was it also possible that I was focusing on this too much? Perhaps. It was like there was a song playing in my head, "Is this my husband? Is this my husband? Is this my husband?" When seeking something so much, it can be easy to find ourselves in that situation.

Have you ever found yourself there?

> *"Father, if you are willing, take this cup from Me; yet not My will, but Yours be done." Luke 22:42*

Lovingly and gently, God was about to bring an adjustment to my priorities.

I stayed on at the Hyatt Regency in Macau, but this time I was by myself. I was coming into a season of intensely seeking God, and I felt distinctly led to take this time away alone.

I had already travelled to probably upwards of forty countries by this point, but interestingly, even in all those travels, I had virtually never travelled alone. My heart was full of butterflies and nervousness, excitement and anticipation. What would the Lord do?

My friends had gone back to Hong Kong. With me now alone in Macau, it didn't seem right to head downstairs to the restaurant as we had done on the previous days. So, instead, I ordered room service—for Jesus and me.

It was a beautiful hotel, and of course, the room service was no exception. The meal came on beautiful china, with a luxurious, rich cotton napkin, the finest of cutlery, and sparkling metal platter covers. The room service staff left the hotel room, and I sat down to eat—with Jesus.

That personal retreat happened to be at a beautiful hotel, but I also remember other mini-retreats, the simplicity of a quiet hour away, seated under a tree by a lake having some away time with

God. It doesn't have to be complex, it can be simple. It doesn't have to be costly, it can even be cost free. It's less about the where and more about how we position ourselves to meet with God. Can you think of a way that you could have a short personal retreat or mini-retreat?

Do we pray before our food? Yes, absolutely. Do we commit our food to Him? Yes. And ask Him to bless it? Yes, and Amen. But how often do we eat with Him?

I did eat with Him on that day. As I removed the platter covers, steam rose from the hot piping dinner while tears rolled down from my overflowing eyes.

My Jesus ... We have heard of the last supper in the Bible. And here I was - with my first supper. My first supper with Jesus. With Jesus. My tears flowed as I met with Him, communed with Him, and He loved me.

The being single thing, the marriage thing—it was too heavy to carry. I needed Him to bear it, to do it for me. I was desperate for a new paradigm. I needed Him to be my husband at that time.

Do you find the singleness thing too heavy to carry as well? I needed a new paradigm, and perhaps you do too?

I needed to say goodbye to focusing too much on this singleness thing. I needed Him to be my husband in that season, and to truly trust Him to bring my husband in the future.

I prayed that prayer on my personal retreat, and you can pray that prayer on your personal retreat, mini-retreat, or even here as you read this book.

"Lord, this singleness thing is too heavy for me to carry, I need you to be my husband in this season. I release the singleness thing to you, and I trust you to bring my future husband, Amen."

I slept soundly and safely in my beautiful hotel accommodation and awoke to a lovely room service breakfast.

During my quiet time that morning, I had a gentle sense to go out to a jewelry store to get a cross necklace with a leather cord—and that the staff would arrange it for me.

It came as a tender whisper, an idea, a suggestion, like an invitation from a dear friend. Sometimes we hear words so clearly and loudly, sometimes as a gentle thought that comes to us. So I smiled and got myself ready. Again, because I was hardly ever alone in my extensive travels, I had butterflies in my heart as I prepared to go out.

If you've never been to Macau, it's a place like no other. Along with the striking Portuguese architecture and the easy-going Chinese people, mixed with Portuguese Catholic influence, there is a fair amount of Christian influence amidst the Chinese culture.

I made my way along the side streets, reaching the wide streets of the main town centre. And there it was - a jewelry store. Hmmm, would they have a cross necklace? And a cross that I loved?

I went inside - and yes, they did. I was immediately drawn to a simple solid silver cross in a display case.

A smile and a few local words are sometimes all we need to build bridges across cultures. And the kindly Chinese owner, with his family around him, pulled up the showcase and showed me the display with "my" cross.

"Ho-mm-ho-ah?" the owner asked. Translated this means "Good or not good?" "Ho-ah," I smiled. Then, a warm "ho-ahh," indicating very good.

The only thing was, the cross had a silver chain, but I had felt it was to have a leather necklace. I held the cross in my hand. I remember casting my eyes up the street, wondering, "Could there be a store up the road where I could get a leather cord for the necklace?"

They must have figured out that I had something on my mind …

"Deemah?" a catch-all colloquial Cantonese phrase, "What's up?" "What's on your mind?" I tried to put it into words … "N'gor lum …" "I think …"

I don't remember how I described it, but somehow, we made a bridge between my basic Cantonese and their simple English. They understood I was looking for a leather cord.

The owner smiled: "Ahh! Yow!" "Yes! Have!"

They disappeared in the back of the store for a moment. They returned with a tray of leather cords in various colours and shades.

"Hi-yah, hi-yah" "Yes, yes," I responded, happy they understood and glad that they had them. I stretched out my hand to the tray and chose a black cord.

It was perfect, but it had no fixings, no metalwork. But that didn't seem to be a problem at all. "Lay yow mo … ?" I didn't know the word for the metal fixings. I tried to use sign language to show what I was wanting. Again they smiled, "Mo-man-tai-ahhh," a classic Cantonese phrase for "No problem at all."

As the black leather cord passed through the silver circle on the top of the cross, it became a necklace before my eyes. The lady motioned for me to try it on. So I placed it around my neck as she offered a mirror to look at it.

Holding my hair up with one hand, I looked in the mirror at the cross necklace around my neck. It was custom-made so that I could choose the right length for me. The owner and his wife cut the cord and put on fixings of silver for my cross. It was made for me - just for me.

Normally, when buying something we consider the price, especially if it is something that is custom made, but I don't recall doing so at all - I was amazed at how easily it had come together.

The cross was perfect, and it was mine and mine alone. There wasn't another like it anywhere. On its short leather cord, it would be easy to see every time I looked at myself in the mirror—a visual reminder of God's gift to me and this precious time with the Lord.

I am so glad I listened to the gentle nudge of God on that day to go and get that cross necklace.

That cross was a visible, physical reminder to me of that encounter with God and the new paradigm I had received. Perhaps God has something for you … a scripture framed and on your wall, a simple cross he leads you to, a scripture bracelet, or simply a realignment of priorities. These will be a reminder, that He will be your husband in the meantime, and to fully trust your future husband to Him. Seek Him on this …

That retreat was pivotal in my life, prompting a shift in me. Rather than the quest for a husband being front and centre, I had a new paradigm. The pursuit of God became front and centre.

It was to be a time of intense spiritual hunger, seeking after the things of God.

Interestingly, by God's grace, my commute on the train in Hong Kong was always going in the opposite direction to rush hour traffic. The crowds were going one way, and I was travelling the other way. Going to or from my workplace, I would be seated, reading my Christian book, while the train on the opposite platform was packed door-to-door with people.

It was a time of absorbing many books: "God Chasers" by Tommy Tenney, "Reese Howells Intercessor" by Norman Grubb, and books on prophecy by Cindy Jacobs. These were my companions on my journey.

During that season, I heard the quiet whisper of the Lord: "Someday, one day, you will be in circles with, or will know personally, some of these authors of whom you have read." But that will be a story for another day.

Courses, classes, and newsletters, I signed up for all of them, growing in my relationship with God as much as I could.

At that time, God brought into my life another special friend.

We had briefly met previously at some social event, enough to say hello, but we didn't really get to know each other. It would be some time later that we would meet for the second time.

My church was having a three-day time of fasting and prayer, concluding with a special Solemn Assembly. Hungry for God, and as a committed church member, I participated in the three-day fast.

I subsequently headed to the Solemn Assembly meeting. Usually, I try to sit near the front of the church to better focus on the service. People were already seated as I walked into the Solemn Assembly. I made my way into the sanctuary, seeking an empty seat near the front.

Thankfully, there was one aisle seat near the front, and I slipped into it. Putting my handbag on the floor, I looked to see who was seated next to me - and it was her - my acquaintance from northern Europe. We smiled and said hello, and reminded each other of our names. It was a divine friendship, just like that.

Although she also was single, she had far more important things to focus on than marriage. She was fully devoted to pursuing God. Do you have friends like this in your life? If you don't, I encourage you to pray them in. God had realigned my priorities and He was also bringing in new friends.

Like me, she was hungry for God. But unlike me, she was as blunt and bold as I was reserved. That's just the kind of mixture that could, and indeed would clash. But God!

A person who is your opposite is often what you need. And if you can get past the clash, it will do you both good. And thankfully, it did benefit us both.

I was already attending every meeting possible, and my new friend dragged me to even more than I knew were going on. She towed me to a meeting promoting a mission trip to India where volunteers would minister to afflicted people. Somehow, pushed along by my bold new friend, I signed up. What had I done?

Surely, we would be the youngest on the trip, probably the only singles, and travelling with a group of older married couples. It would be a trip that would impact my life. God would birth a heart of prayer in me during the trip. One of the pastors on the trip, seeing the heart of intercession that was growing in me, asked one of the mature Christian ladies on the trip to mentor me in intercession. God had divinely set me up with a new mentor in my life.

It was a pivotal time for me. It helped me shift my priority from focusing on praying for my husband to focusing my priority on God. Are you ready to make that shift?

Karen-Marie Gariba

Chapter 4: Pray for you

"No man is an island" is a famous saying that I have heard many times quoted by my Dad. And it's also in the Bible:

Without consultation, plans are frustrated,
But with many counselors they succeed.
Proverbs 15:22

Wisdom is in a multitude of counselors. Do you have some counselors in your life?

This has been one of the greatest things to impact my life, having wise godly people that I could ask for wisdom, and that could speak into my life.

Sometimes we can feel we don't have any, but sometimes they are there in plain sight, it is for us to open our eyes.

You think you don't have any? I'm sure you do.

Pray and ask God to open your eyes.

And perhaps also open your heart.

There's a saying I've heard in Asia … "when the student is ready the teacher appears."

One of my life values is to be a lifelong learner. I've found time and again, that when you're hungry for God, God will always bring a teacher.

I have been blessed to have a host of godly men and women who have been spiritual mothers and fathers to me.

And I still do, even though I am now a spiritual mom too.

On that same Indian mission trip I mentioned previously, God divinely matched me up with a special new mentor, a delightful, on fire for God, powerful in the natural, powerful in the spiritual, mama in the faith.

At the time she mentored me, she held a senior position on staff with the office of the Chief Executive of Hong Kong, and her official residence was on the grounds of the Hong Kong equivalent of the White House. I would go there to meet and be mentored by her.

Surely God is able to bring you before kings and princes ...

> *"... and you will even be brought before governors and kings for My sake, as a testimony to them and to the Gentiles".*
> *Matthew 10:18*

Time and time again in dreams my relationship with my mentors has been represented by me being the daughter, and them being my father or mother.

This speaks to the kind of relationship I have with them.

This heart of being a spiritual daughter has fared me well in my life, and I am grateful for their wisdom, insight and guidance. And I know for sure, I would not be where I am in my life without them.

> *"Remember those who led you, who spoke the word of God to you; and considering the result of their conduct, imitate their faith".*
> *Hebrews 13:7*

I am beyond grateful for the wisdom that they have imparted to me over the years.

I've had it said to me "Oh you're so fortunate to have these great mentors ..."

My response is that they are there, wherever you are. Ask God to open your eyes.

For me, you can plonk me down anywhere in the world and I will find them.

Would you like to have some mentors in your life?

God can divinely set you up. As I shared in the previous chapter, God put it on the heart of one of the pastors on the mission trip to ask one of the more mature Christian ladies to mentor me.

God can put you on the heart of someone in your circle too.

And He can also put someone in your circle on your heart too.

Is there a godly woman in your circle that you respect and admire, a spiritual mom that you can learn from?

Here are some ideas:

Are you in a church? Look around you, there may be wise mature Christian ladies right there in your circle.

Have you been in a church in the past? Ahh, this is a key for someone. Many people move from one city to another, from one country to another, or from one church to another. A simple key to blessing is to keep and maintain some of those precious relationships and carry them with you into the new thing God is doing.

With technology today, people can communicate and connect across different geographical regions, different cities and different churches

Also with technology it is easier than ever to connect across different time zones.

I encourage you, get to know that person. If they say to you, "let's connect", take them up on it. You contact them to set up a time to meet for coffee, whether in person, by phone or even video call. This is a simple key to share with you … take the initiative, be proactive, don't wait for them to take the initiative. If you want to learn from them, then take the responsibility and reach out and connect.

Being a spiritual daughter is something I am so passionate about, and I find many people don't know how to navigate this. I have been thinking of writing more on this, ie, how to be a spiritual daughter. If you would like to hear more on this please kindly let me know.

I have been in many mentoring relationships, both being mentored and mentoring. Only on a few occasions has it been set about in a formal way where someone has asked me if I could mentor them for a certain period of time, or on a certain topic. And those are good. But for me, most of them have come about naturally by relationship. A simple "Hey, could we get to get together …?" can open many doors, and be the start of many great friendships and/or mentoring relationships.

And of course, the main ingredient is prayer.

God can divinely do it.

Getting my eyes fixed on Jesus was such a key for me in coming to meet my husband. As I was seeking after God, unbeknownst to me, He was directing me to find my husband.

I've often said, if there was a sign that read "This way to your destiny" or "This way to meet your husband", we would go that way. But it doesn't work like that.

The sign we need to follow is "This way to God" and all the rest will fall into place.

> *"But seek first His kingdom and His righteousness, and all these things will be given to you". Mathew 6:33*

I'm also reminded of Solomon who sought wisdom and received riches too.

> *"The beginning of wisdom is: Acquire wisdom; And with all your acquiring, get understanding." Proverbs 4:7*

And one of the ways we get wisdom is through Godly leaders that we have built a deep and long-term relationship with.

Many people will just go to a leader when they are looking for a "yes". And they haven't built a long enough history, a deep enough intimacy, or they haven't really opened their heart to receive the answer from the leader. There are many who seek a "yes mom", and "yes dad". For example, they are only looking for a spiritual mom and dad who will say yes to the plan that is in their heart.

I have been blessed to have leaders who have given me all of these answers, but then again, I have been open to hear both yes and no from them.

If you don't have leaders in your life who could and would give you any of these answers, perhaps the questions to ask are "Where are they Lord?", and "Do I have ears to hear both a yes or a no?"

The true daughter or true son welcomes the "yes", the "no", and the "not yet". I have been blessed with mothers and fathers in the faith who have given me all of the answers at various times. But then again, I have had ears to hear them. Do you have a heart to hear the "yes"? The "no"? The "wait"? And for that matter the "do it now?"

The time to build that relationship isn't when you need the answer ... the time to build that relationship is way before you need the answer.

Where can you start building a relationship today?

The reason for the relationship is for the relationship, not for the answer. The answer is a blessing that comes out of the relationship, not the other way around.

After that encounter with God in Macau was the time I started going after God, and my destiny. My destiny in Him.

I had encountered God and heard his call to preach the gospel, and to be in full-time ministry.

During this time I would go to Scotland each year.

I was in Scotland for pretty much two weeks a year. And on one occasion for two months.

During those two weeks each year I was able to build a relationship with my pastor and his wife. So I lovingly say, what's stopping you?

Pastor and his wife. The wife part is absolutely a must, for sure.

Each year I would go to Scotland and put on my winter clothes as I'd go there for Christmas. And it seemed each year I put on a bit of the old me.

God made it clear He was keeping me in Hong Kong to get me stronger in my faith so that I wouldn't be affected by whatever circumstances I found myself in.

Growing, growing, growing. Each year as I made my goals for the year, I sought God about my "where", and was it time to leave Hong Kong? The answer was so clear - "not yet".

As seven years of my being in Hong Kong approached, I started to get a sense that the time for change was coming.

Seven years in Hong Kong also meant that I was eligible to apply for Hong Kong permanent residency. During this time God had given me a love for Hong Kong and the people of Asia.

I had the opportunity to apply for my permanent residency status in Hong Kong and I had a sense that it seemed wise to do it ...

"For it seemed good to the Holy Spirit and to us ..." Acts 15:28

It seemed good and wise to start to do the paperwork.

To gather and collate all the paperwork took quite a while and at last it was done and submitted.

Doing the paperwork and getting my immigration status in order, may seem to some as unrelated to the subject of marriage. But I encourage you, if you are called to international ministry or to the nations, in any way, these matters are so pivotal. Passports, papers, documentation, immigration status, are vitally important. Why? Two reasons.

39

Having these things in order can position you for your destiny, as it did me. Also, these are things that cannot be obtained at the click of the fingers. They take time. They need time to process. They often involve input and approval, from other parties. They often involve sequence too. We need to get A done, before B, before C, and that takes lead time. These are very related to "Positioning", which I will talk about in a future chapter.

I had no idea at the time that the process I was diligently doing there in Hong Kong would be very similar to the process that I would do years later in Canada. At that time, I would be applying for my Canadian immigration status with my future husband, and having already done it for Hong Kong, would make the process much easier and smoother for me doing it in Canada.

My advice to you, my dear sister, is to have your important papers, passport, immigration papers in order. They may very well be a part of positioning you for your destiny.

I qualified for the eligibility criteria and became a permanent resident of Hong Kong, granting me access to return and work in Hong Kong at some point in the future.

I continued to seek the Lord, and I walked in the counsel of my mentors on both sides of the globe, sharing with them dreams, visions, prophetic words and scriptures that God had given along the way.

There was a growing confirmation and affirmation for the call of God on my life, and more of a sense of what that involved.

During my time in Hong Kong, I had worked for seven years with international NGOs, and five of those years were in a Christian international relief and development organization, so I was already serving in the ministry.

But I was sensing more of a call to the church and an itinerant ministry. I was also having a sense that it was time.

This call witnessed to, and was confirmed by, my mentors with whom I was in a mentoring relationship.

I had a sense to go for further training for this kind of evangelism training. The only question was "Where"?

I had already spent eight years in Asia by that time so the natural assumption would be that I would go back to the UK, or at least Europe.

There were some evangelistic schools in Singapore that were brought forward as suggestions but they didn't seem like quite the right fit for me.

So, I found myself clear on the "What", ie: evangelism/ministry training, and on the "When". It was getting time for further equipping of the next phase of ministry.

The only question was "Where"?

With no clear answer coming forth on the "Where", the sense that came was that it was time to go and pray.

Again, this time it was not a flashing light to say "this is the way". But it was just a sense that I was to finish up my job in Hong Kong and take a couple of months to pray and seek the Lord for the "Where".

Are you willing to trust God, and follow God for your Where?

Earlier I had been seeking God for the Where - where was my husband? Now I was seeking Him, for Where He wanted me in ministry? I encourage you to seek God, and ask Him, where He wants you?

The day came for me to resign from my job ...

The international Christian Relief and Development organization I had been working for had been so good to me. From my first position as Executive Assistant to the Director, to now being International Ministry Manager, my work now enabled me to travel around the world.

I prepared my resignation letter and met with my boss for our regular weekly meeting.

It was a hard day because they had been so good to me. I hardly knew what to say.

I don't fully remember what I did say but all these years later I still remember what he said to me, for they were words that would change my life forever ...

As I said, my words were a blur, I think along the lines of ... "Thank you so much for everything ... I have something to tell you ... "

"I'm feeling called to go for further ministry ... And I feel it is time to go for further training ... And so I am handing in my resignation letter ..."

I'm sure it was a surprise to him on that Friday afternoon ...

"Where are you going?" he asked

"I'm not quite sure where to go yet. So I'm thinking of going back to Scotland for two months and go pray ..."

I had been blessed to work with my boss for several years now. I knew him to be a very wise and good Chief Operations Officer and later on Chief Executive Officer. Working together, we had been able to raise millions of US dollars for emergency relief situations around the world.

I will never forget his words ...

"I'll give you two months off."

What? Was I hearing right?

"You'll give me two months off?"

"Yes. If that's what you need, to go and pray, I'll give you two months off."

Wow. At last, I had gotten up the courage, taken the step to resign from my job, and I received this unbelievable offer…

What to do?

At that moment, a piece of advice I had been given years before came to my remembrance.

The advice was this ... in most things in life you don't need to give an answer immediately on the spot. Most people will give you time to think about it if you ask.

Perhaps this may be a piece of advice that can be a blessing to you in your life too.

Wow! Perhaps I could ask for some time to think about his offer over the weekend?

"Thank you, that's so kind of you. Thank you … mmmm, would that be OK if I take some time to think and pray about it over the weekend?"

"Yes, sure, that's fine," my boss kindly responded.

I left the office thinking "I sure have some thinking and praying to do this weekend."

What I didn't know at that time, and what I didn't expect, was that, that weekend, I would have a dream…

Have you ever had a dream from God? The Bible has so many dreams in it, and God still speaks in dreams today.

That weekend I had a dream

In the dream, I was seated on a beach with a black man with a shaved head.

In the dream, he spoke to me.

"Oh yeah, God told me to tell you… "

In the dream, I interrupted him, "Who?"

To which he said "You know … God" and then he added, "God told me to tell you … take the two months option and it will all become clear".

I had diligently had the practice of writing down my dreams for several years. So I wrote down the dream immediately the next morning. You may like to try it. It's as simple as having a small notebook on hand to write down any dreams as soon as you awake.

"God told me to tell you…"

"You know … God …"

"Take the two-month option, and it will all become clear…"

Wow, so unusual…

So, what did I do?

I did what I do. The very keys that I share with you in this book I apply in my own life.

I went to those who pray with me and I went to those who pray for me …

I shared it with them for prayer.

Again, when asking the question, isn't the time to build the relationship.

Build those relationships, and keep connected in those relationships.

Build the relationship, then ask the question.

We were all amazed by this unusual dream, and it seemed good to us and the Holy Spirit, that really and truly, perhaps this was a dream from God …

It seemed to all of us that there may be nothing to lose but to go with this unusual offer from my boss, and this unusual dream that provided an answer.

So I went to the office, and let my boss know … "Thank you so much. Yes. I will take the two-month option …"

Scotland here I come …

Chapter 5: Pastor

On more than one occasion in my life, I have been given powerful, pivotal words by my pastors that have led me towards my destiny - relating to both marriage and ministry.

I have even had dreams where I have been represented as the daughter of the pastors in my life. Those dreams have given me significant direction, assurance, and blessing.

This chapter could not have been written - and would not have been written or even lived - if I had not already lived the previous chapter.

I lovingly share these verses, which have been a blessing in my life. My prayer is that they will also be a blessing in your life:

> *Have confidence in your leaders and submit to their authority, because they keep watch over you as those who must give an account. Do this so that their work will be a joy, not a burden, for that would be of no benefit to you.* Hebrews 13:17 (NIV)

> *Then I heard the voice of the Lord, saying, "Whom shall I send, and who will go for Us?" Then I said, "Here am I. Send me!"* Isaiah 6:8

Do I ascribe to obeying unquestioningly, words or instructions given by pastors, leaders and others? No, not at all.

Two phrases in particular in these verses speak to me of relationship and blessing: "Watch over you" and "Whom shall I send?"

Little did I know that they were both about to come together for my destiny in both marriage and ministry.

Flights were booked, and arrangements were made. Soon I was on my way to Scotland - to go and pray.

I arrived safely and saw my family. They were happy to have me with them for two months and I was delighted to be with them too.

And indeed, I prayed. And I did what I do: I went to meet with my pastor.

Plans fail for lack of counsel, but with many advisers they succeed. Proverbs 15:22 (NIV)

Every matter must be established by the testimony of two or three witnesses.

2 Corinthians 13:1 (NIV)

Having a pattern of meeting with my pastors, from time to time, has been a blessing in my life, and may be something you may also like to consider doing.

At those times I update them on significant scriptures, dreams, prophetic words and events in my life.

Having the wisdom, insight and counsel of my pastors has been a blessing in my life.

It also does something else important.

The verse above talks about "they watch over you" ... sharing our lives with others, knowing and being known, being in relationship can be a blessing in this.

It helps them to know us more so that they can pray more specifically into our lives.

Again, it's less about how geographically close to them you are, or about how often you meet with them, but more about having a heart to learn and to grow, and being proactive and taking the initiative to get together with them from time to time.

I had met with my pastor in Scotland, and his wife, many times over the years and updated them on the words, scriptures, dreams, etc. So they knew me well and knew my journey.

I had prepared myself well to honour the time, as I always do. I shared updates on key events since I had last seen them; prophetic words, scripture passages and, of course, the unusual dream that had brought me to Shetland at this time.

I shared with my pastor what I had been discerning. "I sense I have the call of God on my life. I sense it is the time. I'm assuming it's the UK as I have been so long in Asia, but I'm here to pray and seek God."

He listened as I shared my heart.

And never, as long as I live, will I ever forget the words he said to me. "I believe you are called. And I believe it's time. But, I just have a sense for you: Toronto, Canada."

Toronto, Canada? I must have been like a deer in the headlights! Toronto, Canada?

Wow! I didn't see that coming. "Toronto, Canada, wow, really?"

"Yes, it's a sense I've had when praying for you."

"Wow … that's something to pray into for sure."

This word had not come to him just during our conversation. It was a word that came to him over a period of time as he had been praying for me.

Again, the time to ask the question isn't when you need to have an answer. And the time to ask the question isn't the time to build the relationship. The time to build the relationship comes way before the time to ask the question.

The revival in Toronto was in full force at that time, but I had hardly heard of it since I had been living in Asia. And as for Canada, I'd never been there.

But one thing I knew: my pastor had taken this time to pray and give me a word. And praying into it was certainly something I was going to do.

It was the loveliest of summers in Scotland with my family, a summer I will always treasure in my heart. It was time with my immediate family, time with extended family, church family, and yes, indeed, time in prayer.

I went for prayer at church and met regularly with my pastors, and prayed with others too.

That beautiful summer drew to a close. There was more of a sense, to quote the apostle Paul, that it "seemed good to the Holy Spirit and us," as things gradually unfolded into greater clarity.

I gathered information about the school in Toronto that my pastor was recommending. I subsequently downloaded and printed the substantial application form.

Working through the application was powerful and pivotal for me, causing me to process the probing questions deeply with God—before I even got to school.

> *"For which one of you, when he wants to build a tower, does not first sit down and calculate the cost to see if he has enough to complete it?"* Luke 14:28

Towards the end of that amazing summer, it was starting to settle: Toronto, Canada. It hadn't been on my agenda, but perhaps it really was on God's agenda.

My pastor in Scotland had given that word to me, and not lightly, I'm sure. So, Toronto, Canada, here I come.

When my two months were up, I went back to Hong Kong.

I'm sure many thought I would have gotten over this notion, but it was still very much there. I met with my boss again. I thanked him so much for granting me the two months to pray.

Then I shared that I really felt it was time for me to pursue further studies, so I would be resigning.

With the seniority of my position, I had a three-month notice period. So it was far from a quick process.

I subsequently gave my notice and applied to the school in Toronto, Canada. I waited and prayed.

Those three months were long months. I had heard from God to go to Toronto, had applied to the school, but hadn't heard back from the school regarding my acceptance.

It seemed like a collision course. My last day at work drew closer, yet still no news. Oh my, those were stressful times.

Why do we sometimes have to take a step into the unknown and not be afraid? I've been there. Have you ever found yourself there?

But God is faithful.

Finally, the acceptance letter arrived. Toronto, here I come. But not before a very significant pivot in my journey.

Scotland again.

Times and seasons are so much how I am wired. I knew my time in Hong Kong was done for now.

The guidance, affirmation and protective covering of pastors, leaders and mentors are so important that I am willing to put my money where my mouth is.

Before leaving for Canada, I felt it was essential to be under the covering of my pastor, to be sent by him, and by the church in Scotland.

A phrase that came to mind: Were you called and sent, or you just went?

> *Then I heard the voice of the Lord, saying,*
> *"Whom shall I send, and who will go for*
> *Us?" Then I said, "Here am I. Send me!"*
> *Isaiah 6:8*

I wanted to be sent.

So I went back to Scotland in order to be sent from there to Canada.

My route would take me on a one-way ticket from Hong Kong to London, UK, then 2 domestic flights up to Shetland. I would spend a couple of weeks in Shetland and then take flights from Shetland to Aberdeen, to Glasgow, to Toronto, Canada.

But before leaving Hong Kong and starting my new chapter in Canada, there was something important for me to do …

I needed to be Positioned.

I didn't know it at the time but that Positioning was preparing me for both ministry and marriage.

I needed to position myself, and perhaps that is something you may need to do too …

Chapter 6: Position

I'll be honest—this is a hard chapter to write. I hesitated to include it, but I feel it may really be helpful for some of you reading this book.

Positioning is something very important when it comes to fulfilling the promises of God over our lives. During that season, I had to make a crucial decision. Maybe it is one for you to make too?

Positioning myself enabled me to pivot into my destiny. Perhaps my story may benefit your destiny.

I had travelled the world. And as I said earlier, I was virtually never alone, even in the many miles of my journeys - travelling with cousins, friends, and at times, people I met along the way.

On a particular journey, I travelled with someone with whom I was in a boyfriend-girlfriend relationship. While "on the road," we were simply travelers, surrounded by a host of other backpackers seeing the world. Yet, when we had stopped travelling, we were living in one place.

I'll never forget the realization when, one day, I understood that technically we were living together. I had been raised very, very well. Living with someone was something I could never have seen myself doing.

Interestingly, as God was reaching out to me, something was changing in the relationship. Simultaneously, the physical aspect of the relationship started to fall to the ground, and it was not initiated by me.

I didn't understand it at the time and found it confusing and hurtful. We were still in a relationship and still living under one roof, yet there had been a shift in the nature of the relationship.

This realization came precisely when God started pursuing me while living in Hong Kong. Someone introduced me to the Alpha Group, which is a story in itself. Alpha is a twelve-week course and discussion group to ask questions relating to the Christian faith.

By divine circumstances, I found myself enrolled in the course. (More on that in another book as Alpha was pivotal to me coming to faith in Christ.) But for this particular chapter, I will recount a specific event during my Alpha Group course in Hong Kong.

On that particular evening, I remember my group leaders sharing their testimony. They had been living together when they came to faith in Christ.

With their newfound faith, they realized the need to change their living arrangements and stop living together. However, they were in a situation where they could not physically move out, so they decided to move into separate rooms in the same apartment.

My eyes widened as I listened to their testimony. It troubled my heart to realize that I had found myself in similar circumstances without doing so intentionally. The relationship I was in had changed over time, but we were still living under one roof.

Have you ever found yourself in circumstances that you did not expect? Or perhaps find yourself there even now?

That night, back at the apartment, late in the evening, I looked up to the heavens. I asked the question, "How on earth could I find myself in this situation?"

The response was so clear, so specific, so audible that I looked around to see from where these words had come: "Why do you think I made you to live together as brother and sister?"

The words shook me. The God of the universe had interrupted me - to speak to me.

I know God still speaks today because He most certainly spoke to me on that day.

I repeated the words over in my heart: "Why do you think I made you to live together as brother and sister?" Brother and sister? Indeed, that was what the relationship had become. Brother and sister.

A sense of God's care came over me. He had a purpose for me being there in Hong Kong. There was a purpose for me to go there and a purpose for me to stay there. And He had changed a relationship to be that of brother and sister so that I would not be on my own.

I had travelled so extensively, and at times, in perilous and dangerous circumstances. Yet in the midst, God always had somebody by my side so that I was looked after, never alone. I was a young woman on the other side of the world, in a strange land, and God cared for my safety and protection.

Yes, the relationship had changed, but we were still very entangled in each other's lives. This person was still in my life. We weren't together, but we weren't apart either.

Have you ever, or perhaps even now, found yourself in that circumstance?

This situation prevented either of us from moving on with our lives. It was a kind of "stuck" situation.

It was time to make a change: it was time to unstick how I was positioned.

I wish I could say that this stuck situation became "unstuck" with a snap of my fingers, but it would take several years for me to be positioned to meet my future husband.

During that time, yes, I did move out from that living together situation. And true to the word I heard from God, that relationship did stay as a brother and sister type of relationship. But when you have been involved with someone, and they are still in your life, it can be hard to fully break free emotionally.

The Bible tells us that we are to be in the world but not of the world. For me, that would be a process. God was getting a hold on my heart, but it would be a progression as He gently pried my hands from holding onto the things of the world.

Looking back, we can sometimes see with 20/20 vision what was impossible to see at the time.

God had divinely intervened and brought a change in that relationship. God had won my heart, but my identity was not yet fully rooted in Him.

That season would be a cycle of boyfriends and bad relationships during those years. You may have heard of the phrase, "looking for love in all the wrong places." Yet, for me, it was more like "looking for identity in all the wrong places."

I took action to break off individual relationships, but I didn't know how to break the cycle.

Again, we can easily look back and see cycles that we were locked into that were simply invisible at the time. There is a phrase, "we don't know what we don't know," and indeed, that was me.

Looking back, I can see I was caught in a cycle and needed a pattern interrupt.

Do you find you need a pattern interrupt as well?

I didn't know it at the time, but God did, and ... He was about to rescue me.

The time was approaching for me to leave Hong Kong and eventually head to Canada.

I am writing this chapter to help those:

- Who are in that cycle now
- Who have been in that cycle

- Who have broken free from that cycle but still feel condemnation from it

Thankfully I've learned to break off the "wrong relationship cycle".

There are three parts:

- Praying to break off the relationship
- Positioning yourself away from the person/people ie. break contact
- Dealing with the identity issue that got you there in the first place

I only knew the first two parts at the time.

The first one, I knew from my growing faith.

The second one, I wasn't taught. It simply came to me as a thought from God. I was to utterly not have any contact by phone, email, or letter — anything, when starting my new life in Canada.

I now know that this "re-positioning" was absolutely critical to getting me in position to meet and marry my husband.

The third part is identity. And surely, for all of us, that is a life-long process.

Patiently, gently, with the knowledge and wisdom I have been given, and with the power of the Holy Spirit, God would bring me freedom in my identity. Now I can declare, decree and agree with the scripture:

Therefore, there is now no condemnation for those who are in Christ Jesus. Romans 8:1

I have been free of that former cycle for quite some time. However, I had not yet been fully freed of the shame, sadness and condemnation from having been in that cycle. God used the loving encouragement of some of my editors to prompt me to go deeper and expand this chapter. I know that God will use this book to touch many lives, as writing it has changed mine.

I have since counselled many people on how to "unstick" themselves from similar circumstances. But first, I had to unstick myself.

Do you find yourself in a stuck position? If you're with someone who will not be a future spouse, it's time to unstick yourself.

That season of being single can be challenging. I understand as I have been there. But I also know that being in a stuck position doesn't help anyone. If you are involved in a relationship that is not, or has not, been honouring God, I encourage you to seek God in prayer. He is faithful.

"Do you not know that you are a temple of God and that the Spirit of God dwells in you?" 1 Corinthians 3:16

If you have found yourself in these circumstances, I encourage you to pray this prayer with me:

"Lord, I bring this relationship with .... to you.

I confess and repent of any way that this relationship has not been honouring to You. Please forgive me.

I release the relationship to You, and I break all ungodly soul ties with .... now in Jesus' name.

I declare we are totally separated, and I declare freedom in Jesus' name.

Amen."

I prayed these prayers and experienced freedom. If you have found yourself in a similar circumstance, I encourage you to do so, too. As someone has said, "You can't have your hand open to receive from God if you are still holding onto something."

Positioning involves both prayer and letting go.

In Hong Kong, it was time for me to let go and have no further contact.

Subsequently, it was time for me to let go of the shame and condemnation.

Do you at times experience shame and condemnation because of your past?

If you are in a similar situation, I encourage you to pray and do likewise.

Take a moment right now and bring it to the Lord.

"Lord, I bring my past to You and any shame and condemnation I am feeling ... please forgive me and release me from all shame and condemnation in Jesus' name. I receive Your forgiveness and freedom now in Jesus' name, Amen."

I'm sure glad I did.

P.S. I have been thinking of writing more on this identity issue and freedom journey that God brought me through - the story within the story - so to speak. Kindly let me know if that would be a blessing to you.

Chapter 7: Pursue God

Pursue God with all your heart. It's the most important thing of all.

Are you ready?

In this chapter, I will talk of the most important thing of all ... pursuing God ...

And also of the cost that, at times, we pay to follow Him.

> *For which one of you, when he wants to build a tower, does not first sit down and calculate the cost, to see if he has enough to complete it? Otherwise, when he has laid a foundation and is not able to finish, all who*

are watching it will begin to ridicule him,
saying, 'This person began to build, and was
not able to finish!' Luke 14:28-30

There will be different costs for each one of us. It's an honour to pay it. But there has always been a cost and always will be a cost.

"However, the king said to Araunah, "No,
but I will surely buy it from you for a price;
for I will not offer burnt offerings to the
LORD my God that cost me nothing." So
David bought the threshing floor and the
oxen for fifty shekels of silver. 2 Samuel
24:24

We read about it in Matthew 13, a portion of scripture entitled, The Parable of the Pearl of Great Price:

Again, the kingdom of heaven is like a
merchant seeking fine pearls, and upon
finding one pearl of great value, he went and
sold all that he had and bought it. Matthew
13:45-46

The question is, are you willing to count the cost? And to pay the cost?

"Pursuing God?" you may ask. "Yes, yes," you may reply. "Of course, I pursue God."

The question is, do you seek Him more than anything else? And do you love Him more than anything else?

Sometimes the cost will be financial, other times obedience or other things. Sometimes a combination.

I returned to Scotland for perhaps two weeks before finally heading to Canada.

Across three continents, in as many weeks. From the tropics of Hong Kong to a grey Scottish February, to a very, very frozen Canada. At a price of many thousands of dollars. But I had heard God and did not hesitate to respond.

I arrived in Toronto, Canada and stayed in a hotel for a day before school started. From my window, it looked like a crisp, bright sunny day. However, nothing could prepare me for the chill outside, especially as I was accustomed to Hong Kong weather. What is this land of root beer and below zero freezing temperatures?

I arrived at school, checked in, and connected with two British gals. I also met Nicole from Australia, who became a dear friend and my new prayer partner.

As time progressed, school was going well, heightened by the presence of God and many miraculous healings. His Spirit was being poured out. This season was one of intense focus on God. But was the "husband thing" still there? Yes, but it was no longer my primary focus.

I had my eyes fixed on God, diligently doing my studies, working on my health, enjoying my friendships.

And then he came

I was staying in the school dormitory, following one area of study. He was a student in another area of study running simultaneously.

My first encounter brings a smile!

Interestingly, he had just moved out of the school accommodation. He just happened to be back there on that particular day.

I was doing laundry for one of the first times in Canada. The top-load coin-operated washing machines were different from anything we had in Scotland or the Chinese laundry system we had in Hong Kong. So I had no idea how long these washing machines would take to complete a load.

Every five minutes, I went back and forth from the female accommodation block at one end of the building to the laundry block at the other end of the building. I needed to make sure my laundry hadn't finished and get it in the dryer before someone found my personal laundry.

In doing so, each time going back and forth, I had to pass through the main sanctuary. And there, on that particular day, was a handsome gentleman who made my acquaintance.

On those trips back and forth, we had our very first conversations. I discovered his name was Zak, he was from Ghana in Africa but lived here in Canada. He was interested to hear that I was from Scotland and told me that he had been to Glasgow to minister. I told him I was from Shetland in the north of Scotland.

There was a map nearby. He asked me to show him where in Scotland it was located. We went over to the map, and I stretched to point out Shetland to him, a tiny group of islands in the middle of the North Sea.

He smiled as I showed him, and he exclaimed, "Revival for Scotland." "Amen" I smiled and agreed. Right at the beginning we learned we both had a heart for revival. My laundry was to be done soon, so I needed to go. His friend arrived to pick him up. That was our first encounter, but it would not be our last.

Revival

Going to school in the midst of revival was amazing in itself.

Small group meetings were part of my courses. It was a weekly time of sharing and praying. One particular week, we held small group time outside on the grass (the weather was warmer by that time). As the conversation often goes, with a group of single girls waiting and praying for their life mates, the discussion of our future husbands came up in conversation.

That particular week, "the list" was the topic of the day, something many single girls have composed. It could contain many different things: how tall, what giftings, and so on.

The List

Do you have a list?

Did I have a list? Yes. Did I carry it with me? No. But could I have recalled it to mind and recited it with the other girls around that circle? Yes, probably.

My small group was going around the circle with each girl sharing her "list." Usually a good student and an attentive listener, I was only half hearing what they were saying that day. I remember communing with God, looking up at the sky and the huge tree above us. A question formed in my mind: What was His list?

I was about to pay another cost, trading my list for the Lord's. Perhaps that is something He is also asking you to do?

Fixing my eyes on Him that sunny day, something started to formulate in my heart under that shady tree. It was about to surprise me, and perhaps others in the group. A new list was about to come out of my mouth!

It was no longer this, that, or the other. Now it was simply: "Revival. Revival. Revival. That's my list." That's what I wanted in my husband.

And indeed that is what I got.

> *"Turn your eyes upon Jesus,*
>
> *Look full in His wonderful face,*
>
> *And the things of the earth will grow strangely dim*
>
> *In the light of his glory and grace.*

He approached me

We were at church late one night after a revival service, getting our belongings ready to get back before curfew.

Zak was there at the service. From nowhere, he appeared in front of me.

As I write, I smile and wonder; perhaps he had had a word with some of my friends, who had all disappeared. Where moments before there had been a room full of people, suddenly it seemed like we were the only two people in the world.

He greeted me with his wide, beautiful smile:

Zak: "Hello."

Me: "Hello."

Zak: "How are you?"

Me: "Good. How are you?"

Zak: "Good."

And then he said it!

Zak: "You know, I like you."

Me: In my head: "Wow, Okay… hmmm, what does he mean? As a Christian brother?"

Me: (timidly and with a question in my voice): "Hmm, I like you too?"

Zak: He smiled. "No, you don't get it - I really like you" (emphasis on really).

Me: In my head: "Oh my, what does he mean?"

Me: Again timidly and with a question: "Um, I really like you too …?"

With a big smile, he said: "You still don't get it - I really, really like you!"

I would have replied if my breath had not been taken away. I smiled as the penny dropped at what he was saying.

Me: "Oh-hhhhh…ohhh-kayyy?"

Zak: "I think we should pray about it. We both love God. We both have a heart for revival. Let's pray about it."

Me: "Ohhhhhh… ohhh-kayyy."

In an instant, I knew this wasn't an invitation to pray about going on a date. It was an invitation to pray about getting married. I think I must have held my breath and gone beet red at the same time.

Instantly, the song in my head switched from "Is this my husband?" to "Oh my goodness, this really could be my husband."

I was on my way to pray.

I emphasize this: even when I had most likely met the man I would marry, my position, my posture was still one of prayer.

I didn't change my position to "girlfriend"; I didn't change my position to "dating." No, I kept my position in prayer.

It is so important to keep a position of prayer before we meet our husband. It is as vital and even possibly more vital to maintain that position of prayer when you think you may have met him. This is such an important step. Keep your position in prayer.

Oh my goodness, those next few weeks! We weren't in the same school, but our schools ran parallel to each other, so we would see each other regularly.

He would come to the morning worship time that our schools had together. Oh, my!

I would be on one of the computers in the computer room, and he would come in. Oh, my! Such happy memories come to mind as I write. Wow, God, You are so good!

Other than following God, marriage was the next most important decision to make. Oh my! One thing I knew I must do was to pray.

I continued to be under the covering of my church. I wrote "snail mail" letters to my pastors in Scotland, sharing any scriptures, dreams, prophetic words. But this. How could I write about it in a letter? That would have to be something to share with them in person when I next saw them.

But I needed to share with somebody. Enter my dear friend and classmate, Nicole. I shared with her in friendship, prayer and accountability.

Many times, when singles have, or even almost have a relationship, the first thing they do, is drop their friends. My dear friend, that is the very time you very much need your close friends.

An interesting thing about our school was that you weren't allowed to date, and you weren't allowed to be alone with someone of the opposite sex.

I've always been a rule keeper, so breaking the rules was out of the question for me. So any getting-to-know-you would have to be done in a group setting.

Nicole was, and still is, a wise and godly friend. I still remember the prudent words she said to me at that time: "You watch him in a group, observing him interacting in the group, and you are going to see quality coming out of him." And yes, she was right. I will always remember those words, and I saw them to be true.

It was a time of prayer like no other. It was too important a decision to be anything less.

Emotions

For single women, waiting and praying for a husband can be emotional!

This amazing man had approached me. And my response in my heart was, "Oh, my goodness, this really could be my husband."

It can be hard to hear God accurately when you want something so much - and hard emotionally, too. But it was vital to discern what God was saying to me in this.

I've always been a "journaler." I found the need to write and pray in my journal more important than ever—not only for me but also for when I could share with my pastors in Scotland.

So I had my "Zak Journal," or rather, my three or four Zak journals as time went on. I had a lot to write with my large handwriting in my small journals.

We got to know each other over those months. The conversations were as much about God's call and destiny as they were about hobbies and interests. We were two hearts sincerely seeking after God's heart and His will for us.

My heart grew to love him, and yet we couldn't date. We could only build a friendship, and focus our hearts to go after God. So we did.

My simple advice to you, keep up your friendships, and keep up your pursuit of God.

It seemed we were the most "eager beavers" in each of our schools. The church ran many training and equipping opportunities for the church at large. Frequently, without conferring, we would be the only students, or among the few from our perspective schools, who had signed up for extra courses, like Evangelism Training and Ancient Paths, to name a couple.

Teachers would occasionally choose someone from the class for an object lesson or a drama. Invariably, each time it was front and centre, Zak Gariba, who was chosen. I saw it happen time and time again.

My heart smiles and is full of precious memories. I saw Zak at church nightly when the church was open early for soaking prayer time, and praying on the prayer team, catching for many well-known speakers and giving a testimony when asked.

Walking back and forth to church, we would find ourselves together in a group and grab a few moments of conversation—just us two in the middle of the crowd!

God was drawing our hearts together. Special memories formed at a picnic bench in a public place with people around. Yet it was like we were the only two people on earth!

Marriage and ministry

This is a section added in the very final stages of editing this book, which I feel is important to include.

Do you know that who you marry is important to your marriage, and to your ministry?

This may be a good time to mention another important verse in the Bible relating to who you should marry.

> *Do not be yoked together with unbelievers. For what do righteousness and wickedness have in common? Or what fellowship can light have with darkness?"*
>
> *2 Corinthians 6:14*

As a single woman waiting and praying for your husband, this is perhaps one of the most important things to be aware of.

I saw this verse, read this verse, but it would really be over a period of time that this verse truly became settled in my heart.

Maybe you find yourself in that place?

Yes, being single can be hard. Yes, it can be lonely. Yes, it can even seem that this verse can be confusing and hard to understand. But applying this verse in our lives can also be something so key to our marriage *and* to our ministry.

This was brought front and centre to me in a very unique and unusual way.

Whilst a student in Canada we helped in many duties in the functioning of the church, prayer team,

Sunday school etc. One day I got a call to do the tithes and offering message at church at a kind of mini-conference. Oh my. This was the first time for me. Nervous. Excited. Scared. Oh my goodness.

I sought the Lord and He gave me a very simple word to share, a scripture and a testimony to share. I faithfully shared the word, scripture and testimony, prayed for the tithes and offering, and headed back to my seat.

Soon afterwards I was aware of my friends elbowing me and saying "go up", "go back up", and "it's you" … I tuned in to what was being said on the microphone and I heard that "the Scottish girl" should come back up. So I headed back up to the stage area.

There was a guest worship team that evening and one of the team had the microphone and a yellow notepad in his hand.

He said he had a word for me, and asked if he could give it to me,. I said "yes please." He then read into the microphone the word he had written during the time I was giving the tithe message.

I had never met him before, and he knew nothing of my circumstances, but he shared this word with me. It was an important and insightful word in my life, and I share it here, as it may also be a blessing to you.

A prophecy

To the Scottish girl

Don't concern yourself about when or where or what or why. Focus on who.

Who are you serving?

Who has God sent to help you?

Who does God want you to share your life with?

Who are you to team with to do what God has put in your heart?

Who is distracting you?

Who confuses you?

Who encourages you?

There is a call to the nations on your life. So where isn't the issue.

There is a pastor's heart in you. It's all about people. Who is sending you?

Who are you being sent to?

When you are with the group of people God wants you to be with you will know it. You'll serve God as you serve them.

Your call is to care for the people of God.

The word was about the call to the nations, yes, but in that instant the overwhelming thought for me was that it was very, very important for who I should marry. For my marriage, but for my ministry too.

The guest speaker gave the yellow sheet of paper to me, and, clutching it in my hand, I walked back to my seat.

It was an important and timely word for me to hear. Perhaps it is also an important and timely word for you to hear too?

Seek God. Trust God. Believe God, for the right person for you, for your marriage, and for your ministry too.

Graduation

School was drawing to a close, and graduation was upon us. My admirer fully believed that we would be allowed at last to have a first date on graduation night.

Something I learned very well from my Mam, in particular, is finishing well.

I had invested my time and my love in my dear friends at school, and it didn't feel right to just drop them at graduation night after going through so much together.

I had had too many dates in my life, and I wasn't interested in a one night date, I was interested in finding my marriage partner for life.

Something in my heart told me that this was about so much more than one date that evening if God was in it. Zak was surprised when I said, "No, he couldn't come to my graduation." And I'm so glad he didn't listen—he came anyway!

At the graduation ceremony, I saw him come in the door. I found myself going straight over to greet him before it even entered my mind. I'm so glad he came, as the pictures we have with each other on that day are amongst my most precious belongings.

I went out with my friends for the evening—and I had also been able to see Zak at the graduation ceremony. So I was able to "have my cake and eat it too."

Then the question of him seeing me off at the airport came about.

Again, I said, "No," for I felt God needed to do something in a new season, not just for that one day.

By God's grace, it worked out that he did come to the airport after all. We hugged as I headed for the international departures.

And our hearts melted.

A word of encouragement to you, to those who are waiting, praying for their future husband who may ask is it worth the wait? Yes, my sister, it is well worth the wait. Well worth the wait for the one God has for you.

Back to Scotland

When I came to Canada, I had already booked my return flight to the UK for the day after graduation.

My heart was full of all that God had done during my time in Canada and all that He was going to do in the midst of this new and growing relationship with Zak.

I arrived back safely in Scotland, settled in and saw my family - living in Scotland for the first time in years.

While there, I heard the whisper of the Lord: "Your time in Canada is not yet done."

What could that mean?

Once settled in, I did what I do: I made an appointment to meet with my pastor at the church. The day came, and we greeted each other.

Again, this had been my pattern for many years. Come, meet my pastors, from time to time, update them and brief them and seek their wisdom and counsel. For sure, this is the time to keep up that practice.

I did what I had done many times before: I updated him on scriptures, dreams and prophetic words from the latest adventure. As I completed my briefing, I was thinking about how to put into words my meeting Zak. But he beat me to it.

Pastor Jamie: "Any news on the marriage front?" he asked with a smile.

(I'm sure I was glowing with love, so that may well have been a hint for him.)

Me: "Well, actually…" I smiled, "… I've met someone. "

Pastor Jamie: "Oh, really?" he said with a smile.

Me: "Yes," smiling. "Someone from the Bible school… his name is Zak."

Pastor Jamie: "Zak? Is he black?"

Me: "Yes."

Pastor Jamie: "I've met him."

(Me, in my head, "What?")

Me: "You've met him?"

Pastor Jamie: "Yes, I know him."

Pastor Jamie then relayed the story of how they had met, paraphrased here.

"Oh yes, a couple of years ago, we did the Leaders School in Toronto and got to know this really nice couple who were also there - Pastor Roger and Sheila from Ottawa. We went back to Toronto another time later, and they said you must come back to Ottawa the next time you come to

Toronto. So we did. One day we were going berry picking, and they invited a friend of theirs to come and join us.

His name was Zak. He was from Ghana but lived here in Canada, and he was very prophetic. He gave us a word about our son, that he was physically far away and God was going to bring him back, and that he was spiritually far away too, but God was going to bring him back. Also, that he wasn't going to church and God was going to bring him right back to serve in the church alongside his dad."

Pastor Jamie continued, "That was two years ago, and since then our son has come back home, he has come back to the Lord, and he is serving in the church with me right now. So the whole prophetic word has been fulfilled."

Pastor Jamie continued, "So I know him, His gift, His character and his pastors. And I bless the two of you."

To say that I was amazed was an understatement!

Chapter 8: Conclusion

I started this book with the scripture that the Lord had given me. I believed His promise "that He Himself would bring them together" but even I had no idea that journey would take me …

Across continents, countries, oceans and seas … using dreams, prophetic words and His still small voice ... and even arranging my pastors to meet him and his pastors - two years before he would even meet me.

Be encouraged that with God all things are possible.

He guides us one step at a time.

As I heard God give me each step and I obeyed, I was pursuing God, and He was also bringing me closer to meeting the man that I would marry.

God had given me a dream to "take the two-month option and it will all become clear".

I listened and obeyed and made plans to travel to Scotland.

Whilst in Scotland I met with my pastor there, whom I had met with many times over the years. He confirmed the call of God on my life, and gave me an unusual prophetic word. "I just have a sense for you, Toronto, Canada".

I indeed took those two months to pray, and felt "Yes, Toronto, here I come".

I finished up things in Hong Kong.

Travelled to Scotland so that I could be "sent" from Scotland to Canada.

Went off to Canada to study and to truly pursue God.

Whilst there I would meet the man that I would marry.

I had gone from one end of the world to another, and met the man I was going to marry.

I told my pastor, and I was amazed to hear that not only did he know him, but he had also met him.

And that he knew his pastors. And this had all happened two years before we had even met.

For those who have not yet met my amazing husband, he is indeed a black man with a shaved head. In the dream that I had when I was in Hong Kong, it was a black man with a shaved head that gave me the message from God to "take the two-month option, and it will all become clear."

It was my pastor in Scotland who gave me the word to come to Canada in the first place.

It was there in Canada that I met the man I was going to marry. And my pastor had already met him two years before we met!

Surely, surely, surely, nothing is impossible with God.

I want to encourage you that nothing is impossible with God.

Trust Him.

Treasure His promises to you.

Don't try to figure out how things are going to happen.

Take one step at a time.

Pursue God. That's the most important thing of all.

" ... seek first His kingdom and His righteousness, and all these things will be added to you." Matthew 6:33

The love story continues …

The love story that started in the pages of this book continues …

Zak and Karen-Marie are happily married, and continue to be amazed at the wonderful way God brought them together.

They are the founding pastors of Jubilee Celebration Centre, a family of churches in Ontario,

Canada, and God has given them a heart for the nations. They also love to minister locally, nationally and internationally.

Many more adventures have followed, since they first met at school in Canada.

They hope to write more on their amazing God journey of Marriage and into the Ministry, in a future book, so be sure to subscribe.

They make their home in Canada, with their wonderful son, Zak Jr., who they could not be more proud of.

Connect with the Gariba's at ww.gariba.org

Search in the LORD's book of living creatures

and read what it says.

Not one of these creatures will be missing,

and not one will be without its mate.

The LORD has commanded it to be so;

He Himself will bring them together .

Good News Translation Isaiah 34:16

Let's Connect

I pray that this book has been a blessing to you.

My prayer is that it brings hope and lights a spark in you to believe that all things are possible with God.

If you have been blessed by it, I would love it if you could please kindly help me share this message with your friends.

I have enjoyed having coffee time with you, and I pray it has been a blessing to you too.

Looking forward to connecting with you again soon.

Much love ♥

Karen-Marie

Chapter notes for your own journey

M y prayer in sharing my story…
… is to fill you with faith, hope and belief for your story …

My prayer is that you will find hope, keep the faith, and simply believe that nothing is impossible with God.

My prayer, our prayer, is that in these pages you will find inspiration and encouragement, learn some simple keys for your own journey, and that, very simply, you will find "a love story that will make you believe in love".

Use the simple summary notes for your own personal study, for conversation starters with a friend over a cuppa, or as a small group with your sisters in faith.

Pray with

Those to pray with.

Those in a similar circumstance.

> *"Do two walk together unless they have agreed to do so?" Amos 3:3 (NIV)*

> *"... two put ten thousand to flight ...* Deuteronomy 32:30*

If you look carefully, there will be people around you. They may be nearby or a phone call or text away. Some of my dearest friends are in other nations or cities; and we contact each other to pray.

Promise

Seek God for His promise.

> *"For I know the plans that I have for you,"*
> *declares the LORD, "plans for welfare and*
> *not for calamity to give you a future and a*
> *hope." Jeremiah 29:11*

Those in a similar circumstance.

> *After the earthquake a fire, but the LORD*
> *was not in the fire; and after the fire a sound*
> *of a gentle blowing. 1 Kings 19:12*

A promise often comes when you're not even looking. Don't have one yet? Seek God for His promise for you.

Priorities

Lay your plans at His feet.

His plans are so much higher than ours.

> *"Father, if you are willing, take this cup from Me; yet not My will, but Yours be done." Luke 22:42*

> *"...Commit your way to the LORD; Trust also in Him and He will do it. Psalm 37:5*

Even Jesus said "Not My will be done." Trade your will for His.

> *"Now to Him who is able to more abundantly beyond all that we ask or think, according to the power that is at work within us ... Ephesians 3:20*

Pray for you

Those to pray for you.

Remember the time to build a relationship isn't when you have a question.

> *"Without consultation, plans are frustrated,*
> *But with many counselors, they succeed.*
> *Proverbs 15:22*

I have shared here some of the mentors and leaders that have been a blessing in my life:

Some brought,

Some sought,

Some for a season,

Some for a reason,

Some near, some far.

Seek God for His will for you.

When the student is ready, the teacher appears.

Pastors

Involve those who watch over you.

Remember those who led you, who spoke the word of God to you; and considering the result of their way of their conduct, imitate their faith. Hebrews 13:7

Obey your leaders and submit to them, for they keep watch over your souls as those who will give an account. Let them do this with joy and not with grief, for this would be unprofitable for you. Hebrews 13:17

Position

Position yourself for God's promises over your life.

> *"Do you not know that you are the temple of God and that the Spirit of God dwells in you?" 1 Corinthians 3:16*

There are three parts:

- Is there something that you need to surrender to God, something that is holding you back?

- Is there something that you need to release to God?

- Is there a situation from which you need to unstick yourself?

- Is there something that you can do to position yourself for His plans?

Pursue God

Seek God for the sake of seeking God.

Seek God for His purposes over your life.

But seek first his kingdom and his righteousness, and all these things will be provided to you. Matthew 6:33

Jesus replied: "Love the Lord your God with all your heart and with all your soul and with all your mind." Matthew 22:37 (NIV)

Let's hold fast the confession of our hope without wavering, for He who promised is faithful. Hebrews 10:23

Karen-Marie Gariba

Subscribe to Karen-Marie's blog

Would you like regular encouragement right in your inbox?

In her blog, Karen-Marie shares about faith, family, relationships, community, culture, nations.

Subscribe at https://karenmariegariba.blogspot.com

Mosque to the Cross by Zak Gariba

Would you like to hear the amazing testimony of how Karen-Marie's husband, Zak Gariba, came from Africa to Canada and his journey from Muslim imam to Christian pastor?

Be sure to order his book "Mosque to the Cross: Encountering God and hearing His voice" by Zak Gariba.

Available now on Amazon.

117

Printed in Great Britain
by Amazon

72667119R00077